PRAYERS
for Married
Couples

RENEE BARTKOWSKI

Liguori
ONE LIGUORI DRIVE
LIGUORI MO 63057-9999

Imprimi Potest:
William A. Nugent, C.Ss.R.
Provincial, St. Louis Province
The Redemptorists

Imprimatur:
Monsignor Maurice F. Byrne
Vice Chancellor, Archdiocese of St. Louis

ISBN 0-89243-301-9
Library of Congress Catalog Card Number: 89-80027

© 1989, Liguori Publications
Printed in the United States of America
02 03 04 05 06   16 15 14 13 12

To order, call 1-800-325-9521
www.liguori.org
www.catholicbooksonline.com

Cover design by Wendy Barnes
Cover illustration: Artville

Contents

Introduction

Couples usually enter marriage intending to share every aspect of their lives, but there is one thing that many of them find extremely difficult to share—their prayers. Couples are often too shy to pray out loud together or simply do not know how to go about sharing prayer with one another. As a result, they fail to use a practice that has the power to draw them closer together in a more sensitive, meaningful relationship with each other and a deeper, more spiritual union with their Creator.

Couples who pray together often find that their prayers become more than just conversations with God. The prayers become a means of communicating for the couple. These prayers act as windows through which husband and wife can see each other's needs and desires. Shared prayers serve as doors opening the way to the sharing of each other's hopes, concerns, and dreams.

The prayers in this book can help make it easier for a couple to pray aloud together and can promote a more open and expressive sharing of attitudes and feelings. Such sharing can lead to better understanding between spouses and also to deeper insight into each partner's responsibility in building a successful relationship that includes God as a third partner.

Although written in what looks like poetic form, these prayers are not poems. They are conversations with God written in a form that emphasizes content and promotes reflection and meditation. You can also adapt these prayers to your specific lives or use them as springboards for more personalized prayer.

When people marry, they have the choice of building a union that is as flimsy and collapsible as a straw house or as strong and sturdy as a brick edifice. But even a structure made of bricks cannot stand for long if the builders don't use mortar and cement to hold it together and support it. This is what shared prayer can be in your life—the mortar that holds together the bricks of love, understanding, and concern for one another. Shared prayer is often the cement that gives a relationship a foundation that makes it strong, solid, and enduring.

Our Marriage

Renewing Our Vows

Lord, with joined hands we come before you
    to renew the sacred vows we made on our wedding day
    to love,
      to cherish,
        and to be true to each other
   in good times and in bad,
    in sickness and in health,
      for as long as we both shall live.

Let not a day pass that we are not fully aware
      of this blessed and beautiful promise.
Endow our relationship, dear Lord,
      with a love that is total and enduring...
    a love that will enable us to minister to each other
      with devotion and loyalty...
    a love that will give us the ability
    to respect our individuality
      as well as rejoice in our oneness...
    a love that will enable us
    to attain greater heights together
      than we could ever attain separately.

Let us join our hands to yours, Lord,
    in a partnership of faith
  so that your daily presence in our lives
    will not only enrich our relationship
      but will make our commitment to each other
     grow stronger and deeper
      with each passing year.

Marriage Is What We Make It

Before we got married, Lord,
    we wanted to believe that our love for each other
    would automatically enable us
     to live together happily and compatibly.

We now realize that our life together
    can be only as good and as happy
    as each of us wants to make it.

We have learned that marriage is an adventure
     that is as demanding and challenging
      as it is rewarding and pleasurable…
   and its success depends on
    the willingness of each of us
     to always give it our best.

When we fail to do so, Lord,
    don't hesitate to step in and straighten us out.

Keep reminding us that a successful marriage
    is not just an accident
     or a matter of luck.

It's an accomplishment that's achieved
     through much understanding,
      a lot of accepting,
      a lot of overlooking,
      and a whole lot of loving.

It's a joy that's earned and sustained
     by not only a lot of giving
      but also a lot of giving in.

To Have and to Hold

There are so many people on this earth
    craving to be loved,
      to be needed,
      to be a part of someone's life,
    longing for the blessing that we possess
      and often take for granted.

Let us realize, Lord, how privileged we are
    to be able to wake up each morning and greet the dawn
    with a comforting hug
    and a quiet moment in bed together,
      sharing our plans for the day.

How lucky we are to be able to spend our days working
    toward the fulfillment of goals and dreams
      that are shared with someone we love.

How fortunate we are to have the security of knowing
    that we can come together at the end of each day
    to give a bit of warmth and laughter
    and companionship to one another—
    to be able to enjoy the security of our home,
      the love of our family,
      and the intimacy of our relationship.

When we lie together in our bed each night, Lord,
    let us remember to take a moment to join our hands
    and thank you for the special privilege
      you have given us
    in being able to share our lives with a partner
      who has chosen to love and to cherish us
        for the rest of our days.

Bless Our Home

Bless our home, Lord,
  and fill it with your love and your presence.

We ask you to come and dwell within its walls—
  to live in the midst of us
    and help make our home a special place
      where we can nurture each other
      and help each other grow.

Dear Lord, join us in our effort
  to make our home a warm and secure haven
    where we can come to renew our energies
    and refresh our spirits.

Help us make it a refuge
    where anxieties are relieved,
      laughter is shared,
        and love is dispensed freely and generously.

Let our home be a place where the door is always open
    so we can offer friendship, solace, and joy
      to friends and relatives,
        to lonely and needy people.

Help make it a place where those who enter can find
    a shoulder to lean on,
      a hand to hold,
        and arms to embrace them.

Lord, let this home of ours
      always be a special sanctuary
    where we can feel your presence
      and where we can receive your love.

Don't Let Us Become Bookkeepers

We realize that the sharing—the "give-and-take"
    that is needed to build a good marriage—
    cannot always be measured in equal percentages,
    yet there are times when we're like bookkeepers
    trying to keep track
      of each other's marital debits and credits.

Lord, don't let us feel the need
    to constantly assess and perfectly balance
    what each one puts into this relationship
    and what each gets out of it.

Help us realize that there will be days
    when, because of the lack of time or energy,
    one of us may have to give much more
    than the other can give.

Let us realize that there will be times
    when one of us may be less capable
    of helping and giving to the other.

Teach us, Lord, to recognize when it may be necessary
    to set our own concerns aside
    and help our partner.

Dear Lord, although we each promise to always try
    to give of ourselves in this relationship
    as completely and as fairly as possible...
we ask for your help
    in acquiring the maturity we need
to occasionally live lives
    in which our giving and getting
    are not very fairly balanced.

TWO

Loving Each Other

Teach Us How to Love Each Other

It's so easy to love each other
    when we both feel good—
  when we feel affectionate
    and energetic
      and contented with our lives.

Lord, teach us how to love each other just as deeply
    when we are tired
    and crabby
      and things are going wrong.

Teach us how to love each other
    when one of us is annoying
    and irritating
      and hard to understand.

Lord, grant us the ability
    to love one another
    deeply and unselfishly
      even when we're difficult to love.

Let us always remember, Lord,
    that it is during those times
    when we are least deserving
      of each other's love
that we are often the most desperately in need
    of each other's love.

Staying in Love

When we first fell in love, Lord,
   our love for each other was so intense, so alive.

We realize, Lord,
      that love can't remain at that level day in and day out,
         but help us at least occasionally recapture
         some of those precious feelings and emotions
            that we so often experienced
               when we were falling in love.

Lord, don't let either of us ever allow our marriage
   to turn into a taken-for-granted relationship.

And when we are tempted to blame our partner
      for any dullness that may occasionally exist,
      remind us, Lord,
         that it is the responsibility of each of us
      to continually try to put a little more vitality
         and romance into our lives.

It's up to each one of us to go out of our way
      to make the other feel needed
         and appreciated
         and special—
      to praise each other,
      compliment each other,
      give each other the security
         of feeling truly loved.

Let us learn, Lord,
      not only how to rekindle the spark that started our love
      but also how to turn that spark into a flame
         that will grow brighter with each passing year.

Let Us Learn to Love as You Do

Let us learn to love each other
    as totally
      and completely
        and unconditionally
      as you always love us.

You look at us, Lord,
    and see all our faults and weaknesses;
      you see our pettiness,
        our selfishness,
        our narrow-mindedness,
        our arrogance,
      and you still love us.

You love us just as we are
    with all of our flaws
      and imperfections.

You love us without reservation
    or condemnation.

Teach us, Lord, to love exactly as you do.

Bless Our Act of Love

We thank you, Lord,
   for the special gift you have given us
   in granting us not only the ability
      to help create a new life
   but also the ability to give each other pleasure.

Let us always remember, Lord,
   that this act of love
      is not an act of taking pleasure,
   but of mutually giving
      and receiving pleasure—
   of tenderly expressing the affection and the joy,
      the intimacy and the respect,
         that we feel for one another.

Lord, we want to always trust each other enough
   to be able to openly discuss
      our feelings and desires and preferences.

We want to be sensitive enough
   to always strive to be attuned
      to each other's needs and moods.

Dear Lord, let us always view this precious gift
      that you have given us
   not only as an opportunity for us to
      enrich our relationship
      and rejoice in our oneness,
   but as an opportunity through which we can celebrate
      our loving relationship with you.

Expressing Our Love

It's such a pleasure to be told that we're loved—
  to hear words of affection and appreciation
    spoken by the most important person in our lives.

But most of us don't say those words often enough,
    do we, Lord?

It seems that the longer we're married,
    the more we tend to assume
  that our partner just automatically knows
    how we feel about him or her.

Remind us, Lord, that an expression of love is a gift—
  a gift that has the power to bring
    a feeling of joy and security to our partner
    and a feeling of warmth and richness
      to our relationship.

Love expressed is a gift that can strengthen
  the precious bond that exists between us.

Let us be considerate and sensitive enough
    to always take the time
  to express our feelings of affection fully and openly—
    to kiss more,
    to touch more,
    to care more—
  to say all those simple,
    necessary,
  and too seldom-used words:
    "I love you."
    "I need you."
    "I'm so glad that you are a part of my life."

THREE

Facing Life
Together

Coworkers in Life

Before we were married, Lord,
    we often talked about the things we would accomplish
      during our life together.
We dreamed such spectacular dreams
    and shared such ambitious hopes.

We know that our lives don't always live up
      to those early dreams,
    but it's a good life that we have—
      a good marriage—
    and we aren't about to give up on our dreams.

Let us always continue, Lord,
      to regard our marriage as an adventure in life—
    an adventure in which we can foster each other's growth
      and help one another to achieve the goals
        we always hoped and dreamed of achieving.

Give us the qualities we need, Lord,
      to be coworkers in this job of life.

Grant us the ability
    to always support each other in our labors—
    to encourage each other in times of failure,
    to rejoice with each other in times of success,
    and to be lovingly proud
      of each other's accomplishments and triumphs.

Let the achievements of each one of us—
      the goals and the dreams that we each fulfill—
    have the power not only to strengthen our relationships
      but to make this world of ours
        a better place in which to live.

The Ordinary Things of Life

We don't need opulent homes
    or expensive cars
    or fancy clothes to enrich our lives,
for we are blessed with riches
    that have no limit to their value.

We are blessed
    with sunlight streaming through our home's windows,
    quiet evenings together in front of a fire,
    the warmth of a shared bed on cold winter mornings,
    loved ones gathered around our table,
    babies smiling, children laughing,
    the gentle touch of a dear one's hand,
    the sound of morning birds when dawn is breaking,
    stars to gaze at on a warm summer's night,
    precious friends to share our joys,
    forests to walk in, brooks to wade in,
    brilliant sunrises, radiant sunsets,
    shared pleasures
      and comfort
        and laughter.

Our life is blessed and beautiful,
      rich and bountiful!

For all that we possess, Lord,
    we join our hands
      to voice a psalm of gratitude;
    we join our hearts
      to sing a hymn of praise!

The Highs and Lows of Life

On some days our life seems like a ride on a roller coaster.
We climb up to the heights of exhilaration and joy
    and then come zooming down to the depths
      of disappointment and discouragement.

Let us realize that life is never static—
    it has its ups and its downs,
      its highs and its lows,
      its sunshine and its showers.

We know that we must learn to accept and live with both,
    but there are times, Lord, when we get so involved
      in waiting anxiously for the sunshine
    that we completely forget to enjoy the showers.
Teach us, Lord, how to embrace all that life has to offer.

How can we fully appreciate
    its pleasures and its triumphs
    if we don't readily accept and experience
    its pains and its disappointments?
If we don't try to learn and grow
    from being confronted by its sorrows?

Remind us, dear Lord, that we can achieve
    happiness and contentment
    if only we can learn
  how to find beauty
   in the mundane as well as in the magnificent,
to find good
   in the painful as well as in the pleasurable,
and to find joy
   in the trying as well as in the terrific.

When We're Out of Focus

Today has been such a hectic and confusing day, Lord.
It was a day when things seemed to pull us
    in a dozen different directions all at once.

Days like this often make us feel so disoriented—
    so completely out of focus.

What can we do to feel right again, Lord?

Perhaps what we need most on such hectic and busy days
    is to stop and take a break with you—
    a few moments
        to rest
        and be silent,
    a few moments to turn to you
        and be refreshed
        and rejuvenated.

Whenever the pace of our lives quickens
    and leaves us feeling perplexed and confused,
    remind us, Lord, to always take the time
    to open our hearts to you—
    to ask you to come to us
        and let us absorb your peace and serenity.

Let us be refreshed and renewed by your love.
Let us learn, Lord, how to reach out for the tranquillity
        that you offer us
    so that we may live our days
        (even our busiest days)
            in perfect harmony with you.

Choosing the Right Attitudes

We want to realize, Lord, that having a good life together
depends on our willingness
to always choose the right attitudes.

We can choose
to concentrate on the good things in our marriage
or to be preoccupied with the bad.

We can choose
to see only the faults in our loved ones
or to be more aware of their virtues.

We can choose
to react to situations in our relationship
with kindness and generosity
or with selfishness and resentment;
with anger and revenge
or with forgiveness and understanding.

We can choose
to face life with a positive outlook
and a good sense of humor
or with a negative point of view
and a chip on our shoulder.

Remind us, Lord, that we each possess the power
to make our lives and our marriage
as happy and enjoyable as we want to make them
or as difficult and unpleasant as we desire.

A lot of it is up to us, isn't it, Lord?
Help us to always make the right choices.

When We Complain

We are such a privileged couple, Lord,
> with so much to be thankful for,
> and yet there are times when we complain.

We complain about all the chores we must do,
> all the bills to pay,
> all the responsibilities we must face.

We complain about all the headaches and heartaches
> we encounter in raising a family.

Let us learn, Lord, to stop complaining
> and to realize just how lucky we really are.

There are so many people on this earth who don't have
> any of these so-called "burdens" to complain about
>> or families to be concerned about
>> or spouses they must learn
>>> to share their lives with.

There are so many people who are spared
> not only the worries and anxieties and concerns
>> of married life
> but also the joys and pleasures and fulfillment
>> that marriage brings.

Remind us often, Lord, of how extremely fortunate we are
> to have all these annoying,
>> exhausting,
>>> satisfying,
>>>> exhilarating,
>>>>> life-enriching things
> to complain about each day.

The Seasons of Life

We watch the years go by and we treasure each one.
At times, Lord, we wish we could just slow down the clock
   and have our lives go on forever without end.

But life on earth is not eternal, is it, Lord?

Time is precious—ever passing.

   Remind us, Lord, not to waste a day of it
      or even a moment of it.

Let us learn to regard each day as a precious gift—
   a valuable segment in the celebration of life
      to be lived and enjoyed to its fullest.

Let us learn to savor and treasure each new experience—
   each new and different phase that life brings to us.

Lord, let each new phase—
   from the springtime of our youth
      to the autumn of our days—
   be filled to the brim with hopes that are realized
      and dreams that are fulfilled
so that when the harvest draws near
   we can look back with no regrets
and know that we did everything we could
   to make each other's lives
      and the lives of our loved ones
        happier,
         richer,
           and more beautiful.

FOUR

Getting Along With Each Other

Different Ways of Facing Life

We often tend to forget
    that we are two unique individuals
    with two different personalities
       and two very different ways of coping with life.

As a result, we sometimes get impatient
      with each other's method of doing things
    and stubbornly insist on handling things our own way.

At times we are even tempted to believe
      that our way is the only right way.

Help us, Lord, to be more tolerant of the way
    our partner chooses to cope with life.

Teach us how to always be open-minded enough
      to consider alternate ways of doing things...
    honest enough
      to admit when our way is not best...
    fair enough
      to realize when it doesn't really matter
        which way things are done...
    and kind enough
      to occasionally give in to our partner's way
        of handling things.

Let us learn, Lord,
    not only how to use the art of compromise
      wisely and efficiently
     but to always temper it
      with a generous dose of understanding
        and love.

We Had a Good Day

We had such a good day today, Lord.
It was one of those rare and special days
    when we could really feel the joy
      in knowing that we belong to each other—
      in knowing that our lives are blessed
        with a partnership built on love and respect.

It was a day when we were able
    to feel more deeply the reality of your presence
    and more clearly perceive the beauty of your creation.

For some reason the grass seemed greener,
      the sun seemed brighter,
    and everything appeared to be in perfect harmony.

It was as if we were suddenly able to see more,
      understand more,
      give more,
      love more.

We are grateful, Lord, that you have given us
      the opportunity to share these happy
      and enjoyable hours with one another.

Let the memory of this day fortify us
    and have the power to give us strength
      on those days
    when our lives happen to be
      a bit more difficult.

We Didn't Get Along Well Today

We didn't get along well with each other today, Lord.
It was just one of those days when
   we were totally out of tune with one another.

On days like this,
   our supply of patience and understanding seems
      to dwindle,
   and we not only become easily annoyed with each other
      but we often try to blame each other
         for the things that go wrong between us.

When this happens, remind us, Lord,
   to concentrate on fixing the problem
      rather than on fixing the blame.

Help us always remember that marriage vows
   do not automatically endow us with compatibility,
   that compatibility is something we must
      continuously work at and strive to acquire.

Show us, Lord,
   how to get along with each other more easily.

Show us how to deal with each other—
   how to speak to each other
      more graciously,
   how to help each other
      more willingly,
   how to forgive each other
      more completely,
   how to communicate with each other
      more openly,
   and how to love each other
      more perfectly.

When We Can't Forgive

We had a terrible argument today, Lord,
　　and we just can't seem to forgive each other.

We've tried, but we are so filled with anger and
　　　　resentment
　　that we seem to have completely lost
　　　　our ability to forgive.

Teach each of us, Lord, how to deal more maturely
　　with these frightening emotions.

We ask you to come to us, Lord,
　　and soften our hearts.

Let us open them up
　　and allow your love
　　　　to wash the anger and bitterness away from them.

Let us learn, dear Lord,
　　not only how to forgive each other
　　　　more quickly and completely,
　　but to be willing to be the first to say:
　　　　"I'm sorry."
　　　　"I was wrong."
　　　　"It's my fault, too."

Grant us the ability, Lord, to always forgive each other
　　as completely,
　　　　unconditionally,
　　　　　and lovingly
　　　　as you always forgive us.

Accepting Each Other

They say love is blind!
It must be, Lord, for when we first fell in love
    it was so easy
        to love everything about each other.

In fact, we were so blindly in love back then
    that we hardly noticed
        each other's faults and imperfections.

Lately, however, there seems to have been
    a change in our vision—
for there are times now
    when we find it a bit more difficult
        to overlook the things
        that we managed to overlook when we first met.

Dear Lord, let us learn all over again
    how to be as uncritical and patient
        as we once were.

Teach us how to be more aware
    of each other's assets and virtues
        than of our flaws and weaknesses.

Remind us, Lord,
    that our partners must often
        put up with our faults and imperfections.

Let us learn to be big enough,
    understanding enough,
      and kind enough
        to put up with theirs.

"I Told You So"

"I told you so!"
We both know, Lord, how annoying and irritating
   this self-righteous little phrase can be,
      and yet we use it so often.

In fact, there are times, Lord,
   when it actually feels good
      to be able to say it—
   when it feels good
      to be able to gloat over the fact
       that I was right
      and my partner was wrong.

Let us learn, Lord,
   how to avoid responding to our loved ones
      with such pettiness and spite.

Teach us how to be
   not only more kind and tolerant
      of each other's mistakes
   but also more understanding
      of each other's occasional
       lack of judgment.

Let us always remember, Lord, that nobody,
      including us,
   ever goes through life
      without making mistakes.

Time for Personal Pursuits

We know, Lord,
    that we must always respect each other's
        individuality
      and be generous enough to allow each other time
        for the pursuit of personal interests and activities.

But there are times, Lord,
      when we selfishly demand
      an unreasonable amount of time for our interests.

At times we may take unfair advantage of our partner
    and allow activities
      to drive a dividing wedge into our relationship.

Help us become more reasonable
    about these matters, Lord.

Give us the maturity we need
    not just to be fair
      about the amount of freedom
        that we ask of each other,
    but to be honest enough and unselfish enough
      to give up some of that freedom
        when we know that we're being unfair.

God: Our Partner

Why Do We Forget You?

There are times, Lord,
    when we feel like the innkeeper
     who turned Mary away
    when she came looking for shelter
     on the night you were born.

When our hearts are full
   and they are filled with joy and happiness,
    we seldom think of inviting you in.

It's only when they are empty—
    empty and aching and troubled—
     that we immediately think
      of calling upon you.

Forgive us, Lord, for forgetting about you
      when things are going well.

Forgive us for all the times
    that we have failed to share
     our happy moments with you.

From now on, Lord,
    whenever our hearts are filled with joy,
     come to us.

Come into our lives and rejoice with us.

Thank You for Living With Us

Thank you, Lord, for being the life preserver
  we can cling to
    when we feel that we're floundering.

Thank you for being the staff
  we can lean on
    when we feel too weak and inadequate
      to face life by ourselves.

Thank you for being the strength
  we can draw on
    when our problems overwhelm us.

Thank you for being the wisdom
  we can gain understanding from
    when our lives become
      too confusing and perplexing.

Thank you for being the example of love
  that we can imitate and use
    to develop and build
      a good, successful marriage.

Thank you for being the joy
  that enables us to fully appreciate
    the blessings with which our lives
      have been so richly endowed.

Thank you, Lord, for living with us
  and making our lives so much easier.

We're Glad We Know You, Lord

We can see you, Lord...everywhere!
We can see your glory
    in the brilliant colors of a sunset,
  your power
    in the flashing fury of a thunderstorm,
  your beauty
    in the fragile perfection of a flower,
  your steadfastness
    in the rugged sturdiness of a tree.

We can see your love
    in the trusting face of an innocent child,
    in the shining eyes of young lovers,
    in the warm, caring smile of a friend.

We can hear your love
    in the song of a bird,
    in the whisper of the wind,
    in the bubbling of a stream,
    in the music of a song.

We can feel your love
    in the warmth of the summer sun,
    in the coolness of a spring breeze,
    in the gentle touch of a loved one's hand.

We can see and hear and feel
  your love and glory everywhere.

  O Lord, we're so glad we know you.

Coping With Our Problems

It would be great if we could all lead problem-free lives,
  but we know that a life that is worth living
    is seldom without problems.

We try to face our difficulties wisely and courageously,
  but there are times, Lord,
    when we just can't seem to handle them.

There are days when our problems
  seem to come down on us all at once
    and completely overwhelm us.

Wouldn't it be great if they would just stand in line
    and wait their turn?
But they don't usually do that, do they, Lord?

Help us, Lord, to face our problems with more patience
    and a more positive and optimistic attitude.

We want to be strengthened by the knowledge
  that you are always near to support us
    and comfort us
      and give us your aid.

Grant each of us, dear Lord,
    the determination and faith we need
  to live through the difficult periods in our lives
    with more confidence in your help.

Let each small problem that we encounter
    remind us to be grateful that most of our problems
  are not as serious or as tragic
    as the problems of others.

We Don't Know How to Live Without You

O Lord, do you ever get tired of listening
    to all our petty problems and complaints—
    to our endless and often trivial petitions?

It seems that we are constantly asking you for something—
    that we are continuously
        begging for your help.

Forgive us for being such pests, Lord,
    but we really don't know how to live
        without your aid and support.

We admit that, without you,
        we are often weak
            and uncertain
                and lacking in wisdom.

O Lord, we really need you in our lives
        and in our marriage.

So stay close to us, Lord, and help us.

Come and support us when we feel burdened.

Strengthen us when we are weak.

Comfort us when we are frightened.

Guide us when we feel confused
    and love us when we feel the need
        to be loved.

Trusting You

O Lord, we know that if we have you
    to guide and direct our lives
    there is never any need for us to worry or despair,
    for when you are with us
    there is nothing that the three of us
    can't handle together.

We know that this is true, Lord,
    and deep inside we believe it wholeheartedly.

But when a problem arises
    and things go wrong,
    we often tend to forget to trust your power
    and begin worrying and fretting
    and feeling discouraged.

Forgive us, Lord, for having so little faith.

Forgive us for not trusting you
    more completely.

Let us learn, dear Lord,
    how to face our difficulties
    with more confidence in your help.

Let us learn how to face life
    with more trust
    in your never-failing love.

S I X

Praying Together

We Come Together in Prayer

Dear Lord, you once said:
    "If two of you agree on earth
        about anything for which they are to pray,
    it shall be granted to them
        by my heavenly Father.
    For where two or three
        are gathered together in my name,
    there am I in the midst of them."
        (Matthew 18:19-20)

We come together in your name, Lord.

We join our hands,
    our minds,
      and our hearts
    each day in prayer.

Hear our prayers, dear Lord,
    and answer them.

Making Prayer a Part of Our Lives

Let us learn, Lord, how to make prayer
   not only an indispensable
      but also an intrinsic part of our lives.

We often tend to divide our lives
      into neat little compartments
   and to keep the spiritual part
      totally separated from the rest of life.

Help us realize, Lord,
      that our lives should be more integrated—
   that each part of life
      should not only be touched
         but also directed
      by our spiritual beliefs and goals.

Let us learn, Lord, how to use prayer
   as the thread that weaves in and out
      of our daily experiences,
         constantly drawing each aspect of our lives
         into a meaningful whole.

It is our desire, Lord,
   not only to enrich
      our daily activities with prayer
   but also to make each of those activities
      into a prayer
   that we can share and offer up to you.

Accepting Your Answers to Our Prayers

There are times, dear Lord,
    when your answers to our prayers
      are really hard to accept and understand.

Give us the faith and trust we need
    to be able to accept whatever answers
      you choose to send us.

We know that when we pray we are often guilty
    of having the answers that we want
      already chosen;
    and although we go through the motions
     of asking for your answers,
    what we really want you to grant us
     are our own preplanned,
      preconceived wishes and desires.

Forgive us, Lord, for always wanting our own way.

Forgive us for becoming resentful
    when you respond to our petitions
      with answers that disagree with ours.

Let us realize, Lord;
    that you, in your infinite wisdom,
      know what's best for us...
    and that you, in your boundless love,
     would never grant us anything
      that might be detrimental
    to our ultimate well-being and salvation.

Teach Us How to Pray

Lord, you once said:
> "Ask and it will be given to you;
>   seek and you will find;
>   knock and the door will be opened to you."
>   *(Matthew 7:7)*

Teach us, Lord,
   how to ask with faith,
   how to seek with hope,
   and how to knock with confidence
     in your power,
       in your mercy,
         and in your love.

Speak to Us, Lord

When we pray, Lord, we often get so involved
    in enumerating our many needs and desires
    that we completely forget
        to set aside some time to be silent.

As a result, we often fail to hear
      not only your answers to our prayers
    but also the guidance and direction
      that you are trying to give us.

Let us realize, Lord,
    that prayer was never meant to be
        merely a one-way discourse;
    that it is meant to be a dialogue
        rather than a monologue,
      for the Bible tells us
    that not only will you answer our petitions,
      but you will give direction to our lives.

It tells us
    that if any of us "lacks wisdom,
      he should ask God...
        and he will be given it."
      (James 1:5)

So when we pray, Lord, remind us
    to always take the time to be silent
      and listen for your guidance.

Instead of always telling you
    what we want from you,
    let us learn how to discover
    what you want from us.

Learning How to Live

The Meaningful Things in Life

When we were first married, Lord,
   we really didn't have much
   and yet we were happy!

But over the years so many of our luxuries
      have become necessities
   that now we just don't know
      how to get along without them.

We spend so much of our time and energy
      not only taking care of our numerous possessions
      but often striving to acquire more.
Help us, Lord, to regain our perspective
   and to readjust our often-misplaced priorities.

Let us learn how to keep our attention focused
      less on our material desires
   and more on the meaningful things in life—
      on the relationships we share,
      on the challenges we hope to meet,
      on the opportunity and the capacity we have
         to bring aid and comfort and joy
            into the lives of others.

Let us learn to spend both our time and our resources
      not only more wisely but also more generously
      in the pursuit of making our home,
         our neighborhood,
            and our world
      into a more loving,
         more compassionate,
      and more supportive place in which to live.

Accepting Our Failures

How perfect our lives would be if they were made up
    of a continuous series of successes.

But we know that life
    is often quite liberally peppered with failures,
    and we must learn to live with them and accept them.

Teach us, Lord,
    how to regard our failures not as obstacles,
      but as stepping-stones to success—
    to view them not as discouraging defeats
      but as opportunities through which we can learn
      new approaches to solving the problems of life.

When we happen to fail, Lord,
    don't let us be tempted to give up.

Grant each of us
    not only the strength and determination we need
      to start over and try again
    but also the patience and generosity we need
      to always support our partner in his or her attempts
      to succeed in meeting challenges.

Let us always remember, Lord,
    that with faith in your help
      we will keep striving to succeed...
      for "failures" are not people who fail
      but people who give up when they fail.

O Lord, don't let us be tempted to give up easily.

Coping With Our Worries

We realize, Lord,
   that worrying is such a senseless waste of time.

   But we often do it anyway.

We keep insisting
   not only on looking back to what might have been
      but also forward to what might be,
   and we often get unnecessarily upset and worried.

Perhaps if we'd occasionally take the time to look back
      to problems that concerned us in the past,
   we'd realize that many of the things we worried about
      never even happened!

And those that did
   were not only eventually overcome
   but would have been overcome more easily
      if we had chosen to trust you
         rather than worry.

Dear Lord, whenever we are tempted
      to waste our time and energy worrying,
   step in and remind us:
      "Worry does not empty tomorrow
         of its sorrows;
      it empties today
         of its strength."
      (Corrie Ten Boom)

Teach us, Lord, to save our strength
   for more important things.

Managing Our Finances

We always try to be level-headed and thrifty
    when it comes to managing our money.

But there are times, Lord, when our budget balancing
    leaves us whirling helplessly on that
    "borrowing from Peter to pay Paul" merry-go-round.

There are times
    when all the pennies we pinch
    get the best of us and make us totally incapable
    of agreeing on how to manage our money.

O Lord, don't ever let our financial problems
    drive a dividing wedge into our relationship.

Teach us how to be able to resolve our difficulties
    without arguments and disagreements.

Let us learn how to use good judgment
    in trying to balance our budget
    and to avoid being tempted to live beyond our means.

Endow each of us, Lord,
    with both a sense of value and a sense of thrift
    that will enable us to manage our money
    not only more wisely and efficiently
    but also more agreeably.

Facing Our Fears

Oh, to live a life that is filled
    with total and unwavering confidence—
  to never be afraid
    or shy
    or lacking in courage!

But like most people, Lord,
    we have our share of fears and concerns.

We're concerned about the health and safety of our family,
    about our finances,
    about the success of our careers,
      and the well-being of our children.

We have fears that are serious and burdensome
    and fears that are foolish.

Grant each of us, Lord,
  not only the confidence we need
    to face our fears and overcome them
  but also the compassion and understanding we need
    to help our partner cope with fears.

We know, Lord, that you are the source of all confidence.
Teach us how to draw upon the courage and confidence
    that you constantly hold out to us.

Let us realize that if we face life
    with more faith in your loving care,
  we will be able to face whatever life brings to us
    not only more easily
      but also more successfully.

Doing Our Share

Did each of us pull our fair share of the load today, Lord?
Or did we tend to sit back
    and let our partner do more than they should have?

Help us, Lord, to always be fair enough
       and loving enough
    to willingly help each other with the many chores
      that must be done each day.

It's so easy, Lord,
      especially when we feel tired or lazy,
    to evade lending each other a helping hand.

It's so tempting to just hold back
    and wait for our partner
      to do all the tedious and unpleasant jobs.

Let us realize how selfish and unfair it is
    to take advantage of our loved ones in this way.

Teach us, dear Lord,
    how to be thoughtful and considerate enough
      not only to undertake jobs
        without being asked
      but to also do them
        without complaining.

Help Us With the Little Things

Help us, Lord, with all the little problems
    and frustrations that we encounter each day.

Sometimes it's not the big problems that overwhelm us;
    it's the trivial, ordinary, everyday
        annoyances and inconveniences
    that are the most trying and exasperating—
        the children quarreling,
        the car not starting,
        a leaky faucet,
        a broken appliance,
        an unexpected bill.

Don't let us allow these daily irritations
    to get us down.
We don't want them to dominate our lives.

Don't let us allow them to get between us
    and chip away at our relationship.

When things such as this begin to get the best of us, Lord,
    help us keep them in their proper perspective—
        to realize how insignificant they are
        and to be able to view them
          not only with wisdom and patience
          but with a mature and well-developed
            sense of humor.

EIGHT

Living With Our Children

The Joy of Children

Children are often a challenge
    to our patience and understanding.
They're a demanding and awesome responsibility,
    but oh, Lord, what joy, what wonder,
      what richness they add to our lives!

We thank you, Lord, for all the pleasures they bring—
    for the feel of a newborn baby nestling in our arms,
    for the smile of a toddler responding to our love,
    for small outstretched arms reaching for a hug,
      and tiny upturned faces
        planting wet kisses on our cheeks.

We thank you for toys on floors and balls on lawns,
    and happy, healthy children playing in the yard;
for bruises to kiss, report cards to praise,
    and drawings to display on refrigerator doors.

We thank you, Lord, for bouquets of yellow dandelions
      held up by tiny mud-caked hands,
    for the shouts of victory voiced by breathless,
      jubilant young ball players,
    for tousled heads resting peacefully on pillows
      in the quiet of the night.

We thank you for the excitement of a daughter
    preparing for her first date;
    for the exultation of a teenager
      learning to drive a car.

What priceless joys, what rich treasures
    you give us, Lord...
    to store up in the attics of our memories.

Sharing Discipline

Dear Lord, don't let either of us
    ever try to evade our share of responsibility
    in the discipline of our children.

It's so easy at times to just sit back
        and let our partner take care
    of the more difficult and unpleasant parts
        of this job.

Help us realize how unfair it is to let our spouse
    become the "heavy" in our children's eyes.

Dear Lord, let each of us not only share equally
    in both the pleasant and the difficult aspects
        of bringing up our family,
    but also firmly support each other
        in our efforts to give our children
            the discipline that they need.

Let each of us always fully accept and truly value
    this most important and most precious job
        which you have blessed and entrusted us with.

Teaching Our Children Values

Help us, Lord, to teach our children how to value
    and always search for
        the meaningful things in life.

We want them to search for the beauty
    that exists in the world you so lovingly created;
for the truth
    that they must possess in order to live good lives;
    and for the love they need
    to develop into kind and caring human beings.

Help us inspire them
    to appreciate knowledge and learning
    and to develop deep-seated love and respect for all people.

Let them develop
    a strong sense of responsibility for their own lives
    and a compassionate concern
        not only for the people they know
        but also for those who are not fortunate enough
            to have been born to the privileges
                that they enjoy.

Give us, Lord, the wisdom and the sensitivity we need
    to help our children become good,
        honest,
            caring,
                giving,
        and loving individuals.

Finding Time for Our Children

What more valuable, more worthwhile way to use our time
   than to share it with our children!

And yet there are times when we get so deeply involved
   in our own chores and pursuits
that we hate to stop what we're doing
   and give our children
      the attention they so greatly need.

Remind us, Lord, to always be generous
   about giving our time to our family—
to lay down the book that we're reading
   and accept our youngster's invitation
to come out to see a rainbow
   or a cloud that looks like a dinosaur;
to shut off the television set
   and help our daughter fly her kite;
to postpone lawn mowing
   so we can help our son with batting practice;
to shut off the vacuum cleaner
   and share a glass of lemonade and a quiet talk
      with our teenager.

Remind us, Lord, that immaculate homes and manicured lawns
   are not usually remembered for long...
      but those balls we pitched to our young batter
      and those confidences we shared
         over a glass of lemonade
      and those kites
         soaring high in the sky
   will be fondly remembered and treasured
      for years to come.

Loving Them as They Are

Dear Lord, we are often so busy disciplining,
        correcting,
    and trying to mold our children
        into who we think they ought to be.

But don't let us forget to love them
        as they are.

Remind us, Lord, to always love our children
        just as they are.

Help us succeed at giving them
    a secure and confident sense of self-esteem.

Help us respect their individuality,
    accept their uniqueness,
    and recognize and praise
        not just their successes and triumphs
        but also their struggles and endeavors.

Dear Lord, endow us with the ability
    to make our children feel important,
        special,
            and really loved.

The Gift of Memories

Grant us the ability, Lord, to give our children
    the gift of good memories—
  memories from which they can draw
    strength, joy, and confidence—
  memories upon which they can build
    loving and productive lives for themselves.

We want our children to remember
  the intimacy they felt
    when we gathered together as a family
      to share a meal
      or to sit by the fire on a stormy night.

We want them to remember
  the pride they felt for one another
    at moments of triumph and accomplishment—
    at graduations, promotions,
      and other times of attaining goals.

We want them to remember
  parents who hugged and kissed
    and were never too old to hold hands.

We want them to remember
  both the turbulence and the tranquillity,
    the joys and the sorrows,
    the struggles and the triumphs of growing up.

We pray, Lord, that the memories we give our children
  will make their lives not only more enjoyable
    but also more meaningful
      and more loving.

Instilling Spirituality

Dear Lord, grant us the power to instill in our children
a deep and meaningful spirituality.

Give us the ability to inspire them
with a love for you and your teachings
and a deep faith and trust
in your constant and loving care.

Enable us not only to share openly
our views on faith with them,
but to be able to make them aware
of the security, confidence, and joy
that we feel in living our lives with you.

We want to help them realize the importance
of developing a close personal relationship with you—
a relationship in which they can actually feel
and truly value your presence in their lives.

Teach us, Lord, how to make them aware that their faith
should always be an intrinsic,
permeating,
and daily force in their lives—
a force they can rely on
to strengthen their confidence,
to deepen their love,
and to make their lives not only easier
but also more satisfying
and more meaningful.

NINE

Prayers for Special Occasions

We're Taking a Holiday

We're going to take a holiday, Lord.
Bless this time and share it with us.

Let it be not only a time that is enjoyable,
    but a time that will serve
        to draw us closer to each other—
    a time when we can learn
        to share more,
            laugh more,
                give more,
                    love more;
    a time when we can fully appreciate
        the companionship,
            the kinship,
                and the love
    we have been
        so richly blessed with.

We ask you, Lord, to keep us in your care
        throughout this day
    and to bring to it a special joy
        that we can share and treasure.

A Birthday Blessing

This day marks another year in the life of _____.
  We thank you, Lord, for the joy and pleasure
    this person has brought to our lives.

Bless him/her with health and wisdom and happiness
        during this coming year,
  and give him/her the strength that he/she needs
    to face life head on, squarely,
      courageously,
      and joyfully,
    accepting all that it brings
     the bad as well as the good
     and the difficult as well as the easy.

Help him/her meet the trials of life with courage,
     the struggles of life with perseverance,
     the fears with confidence,
     the labors with enthusiasm,
     and the joys with exuberance and gratitude.

  May his/her dreams be fulfilled,
      his/her hopes remain strong,
      his/her determination be unshakable,
      his/her goals be attainable,
  and may his/her capacity to give and receive love
    increase with each passing year.

Dear Lord, grant that he/she may lead a life
  that is filled with an abundance of laughter,
    a limitless measure of love and contentment,
    and a deep and abiding faith in you.

A Proud and Joyful Celebration

We thank you, Lord, for bringing us together
    to celebrate this important milestone
      in the life of our family.

What a joy it is to be gathered together
    on this beautiful and eventful day!

We ask for your blessing, Lord,
    upon this goal that has been attained—
    upon this dream that has been fulfilled.

Let its celebration
    not only bring forth the best in all of us,
    but let it teach us to fully appreciate
      the effort and the zeal
    that brought about the joy of its accomplishment

Let us celebrate not just the success of this day,
    but of all the days that led up to it—
      the days of striving
      and dedication
        and determination,
      the days of struggle and failure
        as well as those of triumph and success.

We want our pride and joy in each other
      to grow stronger and deeper
  not only with each goal that is achieved
    but also with the love and labor
      that each of us puts forth
    to help make our lives
      and our world
    better, richer, and more beautiful.

On Our Anniversary

We thank you for all that we've been privileged
    to experience this past year—
  for both the good and the bad,
    the happy, the sad,
      the discouraging and the exhilarating.

We thank you for the support you gave us
    when our days were troubled
  and the joy you gave us
    when times were good.

Help us use love and laughter
  to erase the disagreements that we had
  and the resentments that we felt.

As we enter this new year, Lord,
  let us grow in wisdom from the mistakes we make,
    in patience from the sorrows we endure,
    in perseverance from the disappointments we meet,
    in strength from the trials we face,
    and in joy from the pleasures
      we are privileged to experience.

Walk with us and give us
  the love, compassion, and understanding we need
 to make this new year in our marriage
  not only a year in which we can continue
    to lovingly minister to each other
  but also a year when we can build
    an inspiring legacy of love
 to pass on to those who choose to follow
  this sacred and beautiful way of life.

A Picnic to Remember

We experienced a montage of pleasure today, Lord—
    the sharing of a meal cooked over glowing coals,
    the happiness of children playing in the sunshine,
    the joy of relaxing in the cool shade of a tree,
    the scent of pine needles as we walked through the
        woods,
    the fun of wading in a cool bubbling stream,
    the exquisite exhaustion after a game of ball,
    the radiance of the sun setting behind wooded hills,
    the smell of a bonfire and sound of voices raised in
        song,
    the sputtering of marshmallows toasting over glowing
        embers,
    the peace of watching fireflies flicker in the dark,
    the shared laughter, the companionship, the friendship.

It was terrific, Lord—tiring but terrific!

Give us the ability
    to imprint the memory of this happy occasion
        vividly in our minds
    and to recall it whenever we have a need
     to feel the joy, the security, and the love
       that we felt on this day.

A Gathering of Relatives

We gathered together today
  to celebrate our kinship and our love.

We thank you, Lord, for the pleasure that we experienced
  in sharing this day with one another.

Yes, Lord, at times these gatherings get rather hectic
  with children running and laughing and crying,
    everyone talking and joking and teasing,
      people serving food,
      kids spilling milk,
      cousins washing dishes.
We thank you, Lord, for letting us be a part of it.

Help us always fully appreciate and treasure
  the bond that draws us together
    into this precious unit of love.

We don't ever want to be tempted
  to take any of these beautiful people for granted.

Help us learn not only to value each of these people,
  but to fully enjoy their individuality,
    their differences,
      and even their eccentricities.

Help us recognize that we all need
  to care for each other,
    support each other,
  and never fail to offer love and loyalty to each other.

Bless us all and give us the opportunity
  of gathering together often.

Waiting for Our Baby

Praise and thanks to you, Lord,
for giving us the privilege of participating
in the creation of a life.

You must really care for us because you want us to share
in your magnificent power of creation.
We ask you, Lord, to protect and guard
this seedling of our love
that has been implanted in this blessed womb.
Let the baby grow and develop into a child
who will be strong, healthy, and beautiful.

At times it's hard to believe that there is a child—
our child—
actually living and growing
deep within this womb;
that a tiny heart pulsates with life
as it prepares to receive and someday give love;
that a tiny brain develops miraculously,
preparing itself to receive wisdom;
that a small body forms wondrously,
making itself ready to accept and feel
all the pleasures and rigors of life.
Each tiny limb grows strong—
legs to walk into the adventure of living
and arms to embrace life's joys.

In this child, Lord, you have given us
a most precious and godly gift.

For this, we thank you!
For this, we give you praise!

Celebrating Childbirth and Christening

O Lord, what exquisite joy
   to hold this precious baby in our arms—
      this beautiful gift of creation and love!

How can so small and helpless a being
      evoke such overwhelming emotions in us?

We offer this child—
   our child—
      to you, Lord,
   so that you may help him/her grow and develop
      into a good and beautiful person—
   a person who will know, love, and serve you
      and all that you created.

Help us instill in our child
   a strong and responsible
      sense of morality and goodness.

Help us inspire his/her mind
   with an appreciation for truth and learning;
   his/her heart
   with a sensitivity and a capacity for love;
   and his/her soul
   with a deep and meaningful spirituality.

Dear Lord, give this child
   the wisdom and guidance he/she needs
      to live a life that will earn
         a special place in your eternal home.

TEN

Prayers for
Special Needs

We Have a Problem
We Can't Handle

O Lord, we have a problem
    that we just can't seem to handle.

We've tried so hard to decide what to do about it,
    but we just don't know how to cope with it.

Show us how to deal with this problem, Lord.
Help us solve it.

When you were on earth
    you promised to help and guide us
        in our daily lives.
You promised us your constant and loving care.

We believe in your power, Lord,
    and in your desire to give us your aid.

We know that if we ask for your help
        and have faith in it,
    you'll eventually show us
        how to handle our difficulties.

We know that if we wait patiently for your guidance
    you'll eventually give us the wisdom we need
        to resolve our problems.

So come to us, Lord,
    and join your helping hands with ours.

Help Us With This Decision

Dear Lord, we have an important decision to make
and neither of us seems to be able to determine
what the right decision should be.

We have taken the time to examine all the options
and their consequences,
and we still feel terribly confused and uncertain.

O Lord, don't let us go on floundering in this way.

You promised that you would help us
if only we would ask.

You promised that you would always
instruct us and direct us
in the way we should go.

We believe in your promises, dear Lord,
and we believe in your wisdom.

You know what choice is best for us, Lord.

So guide us and show us the way,
give us the strength,
the confidence,
and the wisdom we need
not only to make the right decisions
but to also have the ability
to accept the decisions that are right.

Prayer for Troubled Times

Dear Lord, help us face
 this difficult period in our lives.

We need your strength and courage
 to get through this trying time
 because we face problems that are
 not just extremely hard to cope with
 but are also very difficult to accept
 and understand.

You promised, Lord, that you would never leave us
 alone and without comfort.

We believe in your power and mercy
 and have confidence in your loving care.

So come to us, Lord.
Comfort us,
 support us,
 and hold us in your protective embrace.

Dear Lord, we ask you
 to dispel our discouragement,
 strengthen our hope,
 broaden our understanding,
 and deepen our patience and perseverance.

Give us the courage and confidence we need
 to live through these troubled days
and let our faith sustain us
 until joy and peace can
 return to our lives.

Prayer for Those Wanting a Child

Dear Lord, we come before you to ask
   that our marriage be blessed with a child.

We ask that you grant us this privilege
   of cooperating with you in a miracle of creation.

In reverence and love, Lord,
   we join our hearts, minds, and bodies
      so that a wonder can grow
         in this womb of love—
      a wonder who will be a child to love,
         nurture,
            and cherish.

Dear Lord, we are prepared to accept
   the challenge of parenthood.

We look forward to both its duties and its joys,
   and although we are sometimes overwhelmed
      by such an immense responsibility,
         we are sure that with your help and guidance
   we will succeed in giving life
      and bringing an abundance of love and learning
      to that precious little miracle.

Help us, Lord,
   to bring this miracle of creation and love
         into existence.

When Illness Strikes

With joined hands we come to you, Lord,
   to ask you to use your power of healing
      to cure this illness we face.

We realize that illness is an inevitable part of life
   which we must occasionally accept
      and learn to endure,
   but when it strikes
      we get so fed up and discouraged with it.

We often give in to complaining
         and feeling sorry for ourselves.

Comfort us, Lord, and teach us
   how to be patient with our illnesses.

Help us learn to regard them not as causes
         for discouragement and self-pity,
   but as opportunities for us to learn
      to develop acceptance and endurance.

Grant us, dear Lord, not only the wisdom
   but also the will and the determination we need
      to always cooperate wholeheartedly
         with your healing power.

We have confidence, Lord,
   that you will restore our strength
      and guide us back to health.

Thank you, Lord, for always blessing us
      with your comfort and healing.

Prayer of Petition

Lord, we know that we sometimes pester you
    with our numerous petitions
  and that we are sometimes guilty of asking you
    for things that we'd like to have
      and don't really need.

But, oh, Lord, we so desperately need this.
    (Name your request.)

We have faith that you can grant our request,
  for we know that your power
    is boundless and unlimited
  and that your love
    is merciful and generous.

However, we do realize, dear Lord,
    that you would never grant us anything
    that might be bad for us to have.
Nor would you choose to give us anything
  that would ultimately be an obstacle
    to our development.

You know better than we do, Lord,
  what we need to make us better people.
So with faith in your wisdom,
  we leave our petition in your hands, Lord.

You decide, Lord,
  if this request should be granted.
You decide what the answer
  to this prayer should be.

We promise to accept whatever answer you wish to send.

ELEVEN

Living With Other People

Our Friends

Thank you, Lord,
    for blessing our lives with such good friends.

We want to always treasure them
    and return the joy and companionship
        they bring us
    by giving them our love
        and unfailing loyalty.

Teach us, Lord, how to always treat our friends
    with kindness and understanding.

Teach us how to overlook their faults
    and appreciate their assets—
    how to be aware of their needs
    and how to take pride, without envy,
        in their talents and accomplishments.

Grant us the ability, Lord,
    to always help them when they need help,
        praise them when they need praise,
        comfort them when they need comfort,
        forgive them when they need forgiveness,
        and love them when they need love.

Help us to always be ready and willing
    not only to share our time, energy,
        and feelings with them,
    but to always love and accept them
        just as they are.

Our Neighbors

We thank you, Lord,
　　for the friendly and helpful neighbors we have.

And even though it can be tough to do so,
　　we thank you for those
　　who are not quite as friendly and enjoyable
　　　as we would like them to be.

Give us the ability, Lord, to accept them all,
　　whether they are pleasant or unpleasant,
　　　agreeable or disagreeable,
　　　lovable or hard to love.

It's so easy, Lord, to be critical
　　of those who live so close by and yet
　　who are very different from us.

Help us not only to avoid criticizing them
　　but also to avoid ignoring or shunning them
　　　because of their differences.

Dear Lord, help us to be kind and gracious enough
　　to be able to extend our friendship
　　　to all of our neighbors
　　and to always take the time
　　　(or make the time)
　　to lend them our help, support, and comfort
　　　whenever they need it.

Dealing With Our Spouse's Family

We are so privileged to be a part of another family—
   to have another set of relatives
      to love us and care for us.

Help us fully appreciate
      the value of their kinship
   and help us go out of our way to treat them
      with respect, sensitivity, and loyalty.

Dear Lord, let us always be gracious enough
   to be able to love and accept our in-laws
      just as they are—
   to accept their faults and weaknesses
      as well as their virtues and assets.

Because they love us and care for us,
   there may be times
      when they become oversolicitous
         or perhaps too eager to give us advice
            that is not wanted or appreciated.

Grant us the maturity we need
   to be able to regard their advice
      as loving concern rather than interference
   and to view their advice
      as a desire to be helpful rather than critical.

Endow us with the ability, Lord,
   not only to treat our spouse's family
      with kindness, assistance, and concern,
      but to learn to love them as deeply and sincerely
         as we love our own.

Our World

Our world gets so small at times, Lord.
We often get so wrapped up in our own comfort and welfare
    that we forget about the world outside our door—
  the world of poverty
    and famine
    and disease
    and war—
  the world of people suffering,
    lacking homes,
    lonely.

We don't ever want to get so involved
    in our own interests
that we forget to be our brothers' and sisters' keepers.

Don't let us ever get so obsessed
    with our own success and happiness
  that we forget that we have a share
  in making life easier and happier
for those who are less fortunate than we are.

Let us always remember, Lord,
    that we are *all* responsible
for making this world
    a better place...
not only for our children
  but for the children of our neighbors
  and the children of the world.

Help us always accept this responsibility
    willingly and eagerly.

TWELVE

Everyday Prayers

Prayer of Thanks

We join our hands and our hearts
   in thanks to you, Lord.

We thank you for all your blessings—
   for our health, our work,
   and for the opportunity
      to live in this beautiful world.

We thank you for each other—
   for the life, the joys,
   and the love that we share with one another.

We thank you for our children—
   for their uniqueness, their special gifts,
   and for the potential they possess.

We thank you for our relatives and our friends—
   for their companionship, their support, and
   for the pleasure they bring to our lives.

We thank you for our home—
   for the comfort, the security,
   and the shared joy that exists within it.

We thank you for the world you gave us—
   its beauty, its abundance,
   its reflection of your love and glory.

We thank you for the care you constantly give us—
   for your help, your guidance, and
   your abundant and never-ending love.

Dear Lord, don't let us ever
   take these precious gifts of yours for granted.

Grace at Mealtime

Bless us, dear Lord,
  as we gather together at this table
    to share this meal with each other. ✳

We thank you for giving us the privilege of coming together
    not only to nourish our bodies with this food,
    but to nourish each other
      with our companionship and our love.

Dear Lord, we ask you to bless and help
  the people who are not able to enjoy
    the abundance and bountiful blessings
      that we are so privileged
        to share each day.

Morning Prayer

We thank you, Lord, for bringing us
    to the beginning of this new day.

We thank you for blessing us
   with another chance to love and be loved—
   with another opportunity
     to bring a bit of warmth and joy
       into the lives of our loved ones.

Grant us the ability, Lord,
    to help each other face whatever this day brings—
   to assist each other in our labors,
   to support each other in our trials,
   to comfort each other in our disappointments,
   and to rejoice with each other
     in our pleasures.

Give us the strength and energy we need
   to accomplish what we are meant to accomplish.

Let the love and the care that we share
   make our commitment to all our loved ones
   grow stronger and more beautiful
     with each passing day.

An Examination
of Conscience

Help us learn, Lord, to occasionally set aside some time
to take a good and honest look at ourselves.

We want to get into the habit
of periodically examining our conscience.

How are we doing, Lord?

Are we fulfilling the goals, hopes, and dreams we had
when we were first married?

Are we living the way we thought we would
or are we falling short of our original expectations?

Have we been communicating openly and honestly,
or have we been guilty of locking each other out?

Have we been accepting our share
of the responsibilities and duties of married life
without grumbling and complaining?

Have we been guilty of spending too much time
in pursuits that are selfish or insensitive
to the needs of our loved ones?

Are we being fair to our partner?

Are we being open-minded?
            understanding?
            thoughtful?
            considerate?

Have we been too demanding lately?
            too impatient?
            too jealous?
            too stubborn?
            too crabby?

Are we guilty of being self-centered?
                self-pitying?
                self-righteous?

Do we often take time to listen?
                to be aware?
                to be sensitive?
                to share?

When was the last time we voiced the words:
            "I love you."
            "I like to be with you."
            "I like the way you look."
            "I'm so glad I married you."

When was the last time we went out of our way
            to praise our partner?
            to kiss them?
            to hug them?
            to make them feel good about themselves?

If we could exchange places with our partner,
        would we find life enjoyable and satisfying
            or would we find it
            difficult and disappointing?

Remind us, Lord, to often stop and ask ourselves
        if we would truly enjoy living day after day
            with a person who is exactly like us.